JEHOVAH NISSI

God Turned It Around

DAVID S. PHILEMON

Royal Diadem Publishing Inc.

To the Almighty God, my Rock, Refuge, and Source of all wisdom and strength. Thank You for Your unwavering love, grace, and the purpose You've placed within me. May this book bring glory to Your name and draw others closer to You.

And to my beloved spiritual parents, Dr. Paul and Dr. Mrs. Becky Paul Enenche, who have faithfully nurtured and guided me in this journey. Your example of unwavering devotion, godly counsel, and compassionate care has been a beacon of light and strength in my life. Thank you for standing as pillars of faith and for your steadfast commitment to the Kingdom.

ACKNOWLEDGMENT

This book would not have been possible without the unwavering support, dedication, and talent of an extraordinary team. My deepest gratitude goes to each of you for your contributions, insights, and encouragement throughout this journey.

First and foremost, thank you to Rev. Mimi Philemon my dear wife, Rev. Shina Gentry, and and my assistant pastor Rev. Bright Amudoaghan for your incredible effort, encouragement, and belief in this project. Your support has been instrumental in bringing this vision to life.

To the dedicated leaders of Royal Diadem Publishing, Ide Imogie and Kishawna Bailey, I am immensely grateful for your belief in this project from the very beginning and for investing your time and energy into its development. Your creativity, dedication, and expertise have been the backbone of this endeavor.

I am especially grateful to the Royal Diadem Publishing team— Beulah Orogun, Emmanuella Ben-Eboh, Doyinsade Awodele, Kim Matthews, and Shante Gill, for your meticulous attention to detail, refining every page and ensuring that each word reflects our vision.

A heartfelt thank you to my family, friends, and colleagues whose unwavering support and belief in this project gave me the courage and strength to see it through.

Finally, thank you to all the readers and supporters who make this work meaningful. I am humbled and honored to share this journey with each of you.

With all my gratitude,
David Philemon

CONTENTS

INTRODUCTION

Life is a battlefield, and every believer is a soldier. We face trials, spiritual conflicts, and challenges that seek to derail us from God's purpose. Yet, we are not alone in these struggles. Imagine this: a mighty banner raised high, a symbol of victory waving above you in every moment of your journey. That banner is Jehovah Nissi -The Lord Our Banner.

The concept of Jehovah Nissi is deeply profound. It isn't just a title; it's a declaration of God's presence in every battle we face. He fights for us, protecting and guiding us through the fiercest storms. The name "Jehovah Nissi" first appeared when Moses and the Israelites fought the Amalekites. As Moses held up the rod of God, Israel prevailed. Aaron and Hur supported his hands when he grew tired until the victory was secured. After the battle, Moses built an altar called Jehovah Nissi, a powerful proclamation that God Himself was their Banner of victory.

In the pages of this book, we will journey through stories of biblical heroes like David, Gideon, and the apostle Paul, each of whom experienced God as Jehovah Nissi. David triumphed over Goliath not by his might but by trusting God's banner. Once filled with fear, Gideon led a small army to victory, knowing Jehovah Nissi was with him. Paul endured unimaginable hardships, yet he confidently declared that we are "more than conquerors" through Christ. These stories remind us that no matter how daunting our battles may seem, God's banner waves over us, assuring us of triumph.

This book also explores what it means to live under God's banner today. Jehovah Nissi fights for us in our financial, relational, or spiritual struggles. As part of the Church, we are called to raise His banner in a world hostile to the gospel, boldly proclaiming His Lordship. We are victorious through Him, not because of our strength but because we rest in His.

As you read, reflect on your battles. Whatever they may be, remember that the victory is already won. Jehovah Nissi stands over your life as a declaration of God's faithfulness, power, and love. He has gone before you, and you are on the winning side. Thus, may we learn to believe in His banner, raise our eyes to the One who fights on our behalf, and rest in peace.

CHAPTER ONE

THE REVELATION OF JEHOVAH NISSI

Fresh off their fantastic escape from Egypt, the children of Israel are found in the wilderness in the holy account of Exodus. God's great hand had become known; the Red Sea had split, and the Egyptian army had been swallowed. Still, their path to the Promised Land was anything but easy. Though freedom comes with challenges, they were free. The fight against the ruthless tribe known as the Amalekites, who aimed to wipe them off the earth, would present one of the most significant obstacles they would encounter.

According to Exodus 17:8–16, this story reveals God as Jehovah Nissi, the Lord our Banner, not only in the physical fight but in the spiritual fight and the victory that followed. The Amalekites were a spiritual force driven toward conflict and destruction, not only a physical foe. Targeting the wounded and tired at the back of Israel's camp, those least equipped to defend themselves, their attack at Rephidim was not only abrupt but cowardly. The attack on the Israelites by the Amalekites was entirely unprovoked, a mindless act of aggression directed at a people still learning to adjust to their acquired independence.

They struck them not only physically but also emotionally and psychologically when the Israelites were most weak. The children of Israel were people in change, still learning to understand the scope of what God had done for them. The enemy chose to strike at this vulnerable point, which is a reminder that it is when we are least ready that our spiritual foes often attack us.

On the other hand, Moses, God's designated leader, did not react with a traditional war plan. Moses turned to God rather than calling the army a battle cry. He understood that the hand of the Lord would win this battle, not the might of their fighters. Moses told Joshua to lead the soldiers into battle while he ascended a nearby hill with God's rod. This is a clear reminder of God's might and presence.

We find Moses standing on the hilltop with his hands lifted toward heaven while the fight occurs in the valley below. Though it seems essential, this hand-raising gesture has significant meaning. In ancient times, the lifting hands represented prayer, thanksgiving, and obedience to God's will. It was a visible show of a deep and internal reliance on God. The Israelites fought a spiritual war in which their success rested on their dependence on God's might, not their own; it was not only a collision of swords and shields.

Moses's raised hands continually reminded Joshua and the Israelites that their actual banner, triumph, was found in the Lord alone. Even the most authoritarian leaders became tired, and Moses was human despite possessing extraordinary faith and will. So his arms grew heavy as the conflict raged on; the flow of the fighting changed when his hands started to drop. Once losing, the Amalekites began to make progress. This change was more than physical tiredness; it reminded Israel that it could not survive without God's aid. Moses's tiredness emphasizes a fact we must deal with: our strength is limited, and even the finest of us require assistance.

Understanding this, Aaron and Hur, two of Moses' reliable friends, intervened through divine instruction. They did not try to fight the war personally or take over the work. Instead, they accompanied Moses and held his hands when he found he could not do so alone. This is a beautiful picture of community, support, and what it means to carry the weight of one another in trying circumstances. Moses's hands stayed steady until nightfall with Aaron and Hur's help; the Israelites, driven by God's presence, were assured of the triumph. This triumph proved the might of God and the need to depend on Him in the middle of challenges, not only about conquering the Amalekites.

Recognizing this, Moses erected an altar to mark the triumph, naming it "Jehovah Nissi," which means "The Lord is my banner." By doing this, Moses was saying that God alone owned the triumph. Jehovah Nissi proclaimed that the Lord was Israel's identity and power, much like a banner in combat, which marks a rallying point and a sign of identity. They battled and emerged victorious under His banner, not by their own will but by His power.

Our personal lives speak to us much from this account. Each of us faces different battles, some physical, some emotional, and some spiritual. Sometimes, we feel like the Israelites, who also felt tired and defenseless, confronted by an opponent that appears unrelenting. Like them, though, we have to realize that our success comes from outside of our own will. We fight beneath the Lord's banner; only by depending on Him will we surmount our obstacles. We must raise our hands in prayer, in submission, believing God will fight for us. And when we become tired, as we will surely do, we need friends like Aaron and Hur, who will support us, hold us up, and remind us that the Lord owns the battle.

The story of Moses, Joshua, and the Amalekites transcends mere military triumph. It is about reliance on God, the power of prayer, and the strength derived from fellowship. Jehovah Nissi is a promise, not only a name. Battling under the Lord's banner guarantees that we are never fighting alone and that success is guaranteed.

Spiritual Warfare And Our Banner

In spiritual warfare, the opponent strikes overwhelmingly to sow doubt, fear, and discouragement. These strikes are meant to undermine our souls and cause us to doubt our faith, not only to cause us hardships. The enemy plans to separate us from our trust in God, which grounds us from the community of faith where we find strength. He wants us to feel overwhelmed, overpowered, and helpless—outnumbered.

But the Scripture in Isaiah 59:19 promises powerfully: "When the enemy comes in like a flood, the Spirit of the Lord will lift a standard against him." This verse reminds us that God puts a banner over us regardless of how strong the storm is or how high the rivers of doubt and fear rise. That banner is Jehovah Nissi, the Lord our Banner. It transforms our attitude toward spiritual obstacles and is a supernatural guarantee that we are not fighting alone. The emphasis moves from our constraints to God's unbounded authority. We are not without hope even if the enemy's strategies are clever and his assaults could seem unrelenting.

Knowing Jehovah Nissi is before us guarantees that no weapon developed against us will flourish (Isaiah 54:17). Our success comes from our alignment with the holy banner under which we fight, not from our will. The apostle Paul echoes the truth of this divine victory in Romans 8:37 when he boldly states, "In all these things we are more than conquerors through Him who loved us." This declares firmly that our position as conquerors results from our fight under the banner of Jehovah Nissi, not from our capacity.

The best emblem of this triumph is Christ's cross. Jesus broke sin, death, and all the powers of darkness at the cross. His victory was for all of us as much as for Himself. This triumph is a gift we walk in by faith; we do not have to earn it. Jesus at Calvary already won every war we fight today; when we line up with Him, the power of His victory permeates every sphere of our lives. It's about realizing that we are winners thanks to what Jesus accomplished. It's not about trying harder or fighting with our might. This helps us to see from the struggle to the triumph perspective, even in the middle of the storm.

The declaration of Jehovah Nissi also invites us to lead lives of ongoing reliance on God. We, too, must be steadfast in our relationship with God via prayer, worship, and obedience, much as Moses had to keep his hands raised for the length of the battle. Moses's hands raised toward heaven represented his dependence on God's might; when he grew fatigued and lowered them, the enemy started to win. This is a striking warning that the enemy advances when we become tired of our faith and spiritual practices or try to depend on our strength. But we are not supposed to fight by ourselves. When we feel weak, we have the strength of God and the encouragement of other Christians, much as Aaron and Hur accompanied Moses to support him. We can stand up in faith together.

In other words, victory is about tenaciously depending on God's strength and leaning on the community of faith He has given, not about never feeling weak. Victory is guaranteed when we rely on God, raise our hands in surrender, and let others help us when we are tired. We must remember that the Lord owns the fight; defeat is not an option beneath His banner. Jehovah Nissi guides us; we shall triumph as long as we believe in Him and keep close to the heavenly source of our strength.

Jehovah Nissi In The Life Of A Believer

Jehovah Nissi is a living, breathing reality that affects the entirety of every believer's path today, not just a historical footnote. We come into conflicts on several fronts as we navigate the challenges associated with our faith. These highly personal battles rock us to our roots, not far-off, abstract wars. We encounter challenges to our convictions and tests of will daily. Maybe it's a personal failure or incompetence threatening to define us or a career setback causing us to doubt our direction.

Our families struggle with issues that test our boundaries and sour relationships. It might be a prodigal child, a failing marriage, or the weight of looking after aging parents. On our spiritual journey, we encounter challenges that undermine our faith, therefore throwing uncertainty on God's goodness and our value. Jehovah Nissi is our unflinching flag amid these storms. Imagine a battlefield, uncertainty ruling and smoke whirling. Soldiers search for their banner, a gathering point that provides direction and clarity in such anarchy. For us, Jehovah Nissi is that. He is a present aid, not only an idea or a far-off god during difficult times.

To this banner, we must look when the noise of life threatens to silence His voice and when events seem to be working against us. Our uniting power is Jehovah Nissi, which gives the disjointed bits of our life consistency. In Him, our suffering gets direction, our suffering finds purpose, and our weakness becomes the stage for His might. He is our strength, not only the means to help us to conquer. He is ready to empower us, raise us above the tumult, and offer us a viewpoint that goes beyond our limited human knowledge in every trial, every difficulty, and every attack.

Pause for a moment and think of the difficulties you now encounter. Spend some time considering the conflicts you are now fighting in your life. Maybe you conflict with a sin that seems to be strangling your life. Whenever you believe you have made progress, it pulls back and makes you ashamed and demoralized. Perhaps you are struggling with anxiety and fear that paralyze you and rob you of happiness and peace. Every step forward seems like a great effort; the future looms like a black cloud. For others, the fight can be for bodily well-being. Or You are battling chronic pain that saps your strength daily or a diagnosis that might define your life.

Maybe your battlefield is found in your relationships. You are trying to close a distance with a child who has become far-off or preserve a marriage that looks to be beyond repair. Under these circumstances, one is all too prone to feeling overwhelmed. The opposition seems to have the upper hand; hence, defeat feels feasible and natural. But we must remember the vital lesson from the Amalekites even in these dark times. Their narrative is not only old history; it's vivid imagery for our present realities. Remember how the Israelites were failing despite more power or strategy? But their cooperation with Jehovah Nissi brought about their success. And as Moses raised his hands to represent their reliance on God, the war changed to their advantage. This striking visual reminds us that our connection to the source of all strength defines our success in life's challenges rather than our own will.

How, therefore, may we apply this knowledge to our daily lives? It begins in a humble and subservient posture. Raise your hands in prayer as a statement of your complete reliance on God, not as a religious ceremony. Those times when you feel most weak, or the enemy seems to be advancing are when you should most ardently confess the promises of God over your life. Speak them out loudly. Let them speak to your spirit. Let them wash out the enemy's lies. Say you are more than a conqueror through Christ. Declare that no weapon created to target you will flourish. Say you have enough grace from God, and His strength is perfect in your weakness. Get strong, knowing He is battling for you. This is a rock-solid fact based on God's nature, not wishful thinking or naive optimism.

Jehovah Nissi actively participates in your conflicts, works behind the scenes, plans events, and helps you to overcome them; he is not only a passive witness of your hardships. Moreover, the disclosure of Jehovah Nissi reminds us very much of the vital role community plays in our spiritual battle. Supported by Aaron and Hur, Moses presents a stunning picture of the interdependence God has created for His people. We were never supposed to fight our battles alone, much as Moses could not maintain the posture of supplication by himself. In its best sense, the church is a living, breathing community of Christians gathered under the banner of

Christ, not only a building or an institution. It's a support system divinely arranged to give responsibility, confidence, and strength. Standing together, connected arm in arm with our brothers and sisters in Christ, we show a great force against which the gates of hell cannot prevail.

This oneness is about hearts tied together in prayer, minds oriented in purpose, and spirits united in faith. It is not only about physical presence. It's about holding one another's weight, translating words of life into deadly circumstances, and filling in for people too frail to stand on their own. Adopting this kind of society helps us create an environment where the enemy's plans are destroyed rather than only hampered.

The Victory of the Cross

A deeper exploration of Jehovah Nissi reveals its final embodiment in the cross of Christ. Should the banner Moses raised be a foreshadowing, then the crucifixion serves as the fulfillment, a benchmark for all humanity to see. It is an everlasting statement that the most brutal fight has been won. Jesus was doing considerably more than just commemorating the end of His earthly suffering when he spoke those potent words, "It is finished." Declaring the whole and permanent defeat of the enemy, those three words rang across time and eternity.

The cross is our flag of triumph, a rallying point for Christians of many centuries and cultures, not only a sign of sacrifice. We advance in faith under this banner. Every action we take is a statement of the already guaranteed victory. The cross modifies everything. It changes our view from a terrible struggle to assured success. We fight for success; we no longer fight for it. This slight change in perspective can transform our approach to all elements of our life. We must let this great mystery of God as Jehovah Nissi infiltrate every thread of our existence. Let it sink firmly into your spirit so you thrive rather than merely exist. You are more than a victor through Christ who loves you; you are not barely surviving.

Though the outcome has already been decided, the battles you confront could be intense and some of the toughest you have ever faced. In Christ, we have the unquestionable confidence that we can remain steady whatever comes our way. Our feet are set on the firm rock of God's faithfulness; hence, when the winds of adversity scream, and the waves of trouble smash against us, we are not moved. The Lord our Banner, Jehovah Nissi, is not a far-off God but a present reality always by our side. As we keep discovering the several facets of Jehovah Nissi throughout this book, I pray that this insight will sink firmly into your heart. May it be a life-breathing truth that enables you to walk in the victory that has been assured for you, not only head knowledge.

In any case, raise your gaze to the banner. Look not on the scale of your difficulties but on the glory of your God. Trust in the Lord's unwavering love, a love so great and deep that it brought Him to the cross for you. Even when your strength fails, let this love be the gasoline driving you on. Proceed with the serene assurance that results from realizing the Lord's battle is not yours. You are not battling alone; you are not fighting in useless futility. Jehovah Nissi stands for God as your banner, soaring above the muck of daily existence. He shields you from the opponent's scorching arrows like a guardian. And He is your victory, guaranteeing that you will finally stand triumphant. Lift your hands, raise your voice, and march beneath His banner. Already yours is the triumph; go on and seize it!

CHAPTER TWO

PROPHETIC VOICES AND THE BANNER OF GOD

God has always spoken to His people from the birth of creation, leading, directing, and consoling them through the words of His prophets. Reminding humanity of God's immutable truth, these trans-generational prophetic voices have been divine messengers crossing the distance between heaven and earth. These voices are remarkable in that they transcended their era. Their messages have reverberated across generations to appeal to people's hearts now.

It wasn't just perfect people who were selected to be prophets. Many of them battled their uncertainty, shortcomings, and restrictions. However, their commitment to being vessels for God's word and compliance with His call distinguished them, even if it meant running risk, mockery, or suffering. Though their work was not simple, they performed their duty faithfully, knowing they were given messages meant to span time and space. Inspired by the Holy Spirit, these prophets speak timeless words. They talk to us now, and, like they did for those who first heard them centuries ago, they provide direction and insight into our spiritual path.

In the Bible, men and women who stood as prophetic pillars in their time, imparting contemporary and ageless teachings abound. For instance, Isaiah's grand vision of the suffering servant went beyond a prophecy for his generation. Years before His birth, it was a prophecy of the approaching Messiah, Jesus Christ. Isaiah's words still ring true today about the redeeming effort of Jesus and the atonement He presents. Reminded of the strength of God's promises, Isaiah's message of hope and rescue is as pertinent today as it was then.

Comparably, the prophet Ezekiel created a striking picture of resurrection and healing using his vision of the valley of dry bones. His message addresses all of us about God's capacity to give life to circumstances that seem dead or hopeless, transcending the mere restoration of Israel. Ezekiel's prophecy inspires our faith, reminding us that God can restore what has been damaged and bring fresh life, even if our situation may seem bleak. These prophetic voices have permanently changed history; their words inspire trust, hope, and a better knowledge of God's character.

God raised these prophetic voices to announce His will and guide His people over times of crisis, uncertainty, and transformation. More significantly than just foretelling future events, they exposed the profound realities of God. Encouraging individuals toward confession, righteousness, and a rebuilt relationship with their Creator, their goal was to call them back to God. This was no simple role. Often, the words they presented were hard facts individuals did not want to hear. Still, these prophets stayed constant in their dedication to God's call. Though it meant standing alone, they spoke boldly and without fear of the repercussions. Though many went through rejection, pain, and adversity, their loyalty to God was unflinching.

Their sacrifice has paid off. Today, we are the recipients of their ministry. The words they used centuries ago still direct us and offer a clear road back to God when we are unsure and in upheaval. Their bravery and dedication have created a legacy that still shapes our spiritual path. These men and women of God spoke prophetic words meant for all time, not only for their day. And that is also why, though it was penned thousands of years ago, the Bible is still relevant since it is not only a historical record. Comprising timeless pertinent principles to every generation, it is the living Word of God.

Reading the prophecies of Isaiah, Ezekiel, Jeremiah, or any of the prophets is not only reading about events from the past. Today, we are hearing the voice of God speaking into our lives. Being divinely inspired gives their remarks an eternal appeal. The prophetic words of Scripture provide us responses that are as pertinent now as they were when they were first delivered, whether our needs are for direction, comfort, or understanding. Because the Bible captures God's immutable character, it remains a source of life and direction. His word is alive, and as we interact with the Scriptures, we discover that God still speaks via His prophets, providing hope for the future and knowledge for our present situation.

When we examine the part prophetic voices play in the framework of Jehovah Nissi, it is clear that these prophets served under God's banner. They were empowered by the heavenly authority of Jehovah Nissi, the Lord, their Banner, not speaking from their jurisdiction. Over their lives and missions, this banner stood for God's favor, protection, and direction. It was a statement that they were not working alone toward their goals. By leading them in their prophetic tasks and waging their conflicts, Jehovah Nissi went before them.

This banner of God's presence guaranteed them that God was with them, guiding their words and deeds regardless of the opposition they encountered. Their confidence came from the God who called them, not their capacity. This divine banner covered the prophets of old, and it covers us also now. They trust that we are never alone as long as we fly under His banner. Hence, we are invited to live under the protection and direction of Jehovah Nissi, where victory is ensured.

The Power Of Alignment With God's Banner

God also raises a banner above a prophetic voice to indicate His favor and protection. This holy banner is a powerful revelation of God's presence, strength, and will in the prophet's life, not only an abstract emblem. For instance, when God invited Ezekiel to prophesy to the nation of Israel, He did it well, aware of the challenges Ezekiel would encounter. Knowing that Ezekiel's road would not be simple, God assigned him to speak to rebellious and tenacious people. "Do not be scared of them or their words," he advised Ezekiel ahead of time, stating, "You live among scorpions, and briers and thorns are all around you. "Do not be afraid of what they say or be terrified by them," Ezekiel 2:6 advises. These were promises of God's support and protection, not only directions.

The prophet Ezekiel stayed faithful to his calling in the face of growing resistance, believing that Jehovah Nissi, the Lord his Banner, was with him every step of the way. In Covering Ezekiel, the banner manifested divine might, clearly stating that no human resistance could overcome God's will. Not only did this holy banner above Ezekiel's life serve his safety, but it also clearly indicated God's support of his work. For Ezekiel and those who heard him, it served as a continual comfort as God was with him regardless of how strong the resistance or complicated the tasks seemed. Eventually, his purposes would take center stage irrespective of any developed challenges. This same fact holds for each of us now. We are also covered by His banner, Jehovah Nissi, when we align ourselves with God's desire and purpose.

This banner also powerfully represents God's favor, protection, and direction over our lives. We are not traveling this road alone; this truth makes the heart glad. More significantly, this unity with God's flag affects not only our own lives. It can affect others around us and even help to determine the course of subsequent generations. Knowing God is battling for us even if we cannot see the whole picture. Living under His banner means bringing His presence and authority into every circumstance.

Think of the broad influence the prophets had on the next generations. Their compliance with God's command affected not just their personal lives or nearby surroundings but also the path of history. Isaiah's prophecies, for example, were not only for his day. His remarks about the approaching Messiah helped to define Israel's expectations and set the path for Christ's appearance centuries later. Isaiah was not only addressing a modern problem when he discussed the suffering of the servant; he was pointing ahead to the ultimate salvation through Christ Jesus. His compliance has a ripple effect that is seen even now as his prophecies still inspire hope and help us to define salvation.

Likewise, Ezekiel's ideas of atonement were more than merely solace for exiles. They pointed toward God's ability to bring life to what seems dead and inspired hope in a nation gone broke. Though anchored in their historical settings, these prophetic voices remind us that His intentions span time and situation and inspire faith in God's everlasting designs. These prophets shared God's heart and invited people to atonement, righteousness, and closer contact with God, not only foreseeing the future. At tremendous personal sacrifice, their compliance with God's command often laid a basis of faith that the next generations may inherit.

For each of us now, this same fact holds. Our immediate surroundings and the lives of people who follow us could be shaped by our obedience or alignment to God and our readiness to answer His calling. The tradition of the prophets reminds us powerfully that our life becomes part of something far more than ourselves when we decide to walk under God's banner. Though we might not always see the whole effect of our obedience, we can rely on God to guide our lives into His grand redemptive scheme. Saying "yes" to God's call is more than reacting to a passing feeling of obligation or a transient need. We are entering the incredible story of God's redemptive purpose, spanning and transcending time.

Though our lives appear minor in the grand scheme of things, they become vital to the more remarkable story and plan God is authoring. Beginning with the prophets of older men and women like Isaiah and Ezekiel, this narrative runs ahead into the future as God keeps His promises fulfilled. Aligning ourselves with God's banner has the beauty of helping us to link to this timeless story. It is about what God can accomplish over our lives for the next generations, not only about what He can do here. Under the banner of Jehovah Nissi, we can live with hope, faith, and atonement for the future, knowing that our compliance and alignment or commitment now will leave a legacy for subsequent generations.

Aligning yourself with God's banner guarantees our protection and direction and helps us contribute to a legacy beyond our lives. Old prophets sensed this, and their response to God's call still shapes our conception of faith. Likewise, our reverence and faith in God can motivate and influence others who follow us by directing them to the unbroken love and fidelity of Jehovah Nissi. In this sense, we become players in God's will and messengers of His banner, announcing His triumph and presence to the surroundings. God Himself is our banner, guiding, fighting for us, and ensuring His objectives will finally come first. Once again. We are never alone in this world.

The Prophetic Legacy Of Jehovah Nissi

The legacy of the prophets serves as a potent reminder of what results when familiar people align with God's will. Men and women just like us, with their worries, shortcomings, and difficulties, yet they became remarkable tools in God's hand. Their readiness to let God lead them in whatever they did and to trust in His banner set them apart. Their lives were not their own, and they knew a significant and profound truth about this. They belonged to something far more than themselves; they were a divine blueprint spanning decades and generations. Understanding this, they could not fail beneath God's banner; hence, they could not fail in persecution, adversity, or even death. This faith is what we find in prophets such as Elijah, Jeremiah, and Isaiah, who, understanding that their strength came from God rather than from themselves, stood firm in the face of fantastic adversity, and today, their names still echo through history.

We inherit this same legacy right now. Though we might feel inadequate or too ordinary to have an influence, as we line up with God's banner, we join the prophetic lineage handed down through centuries. Our call is to be prophetic voices in our age, not only to be receivers of the prophetic utterances delivered in the past. Like the prophets, we are invited to announce the truth of God's Word and to stand firm even in front of resistance. This is not simple because walking according to God's will requires faith and bravery.

The beauty of it all is that knowing Jehovah Nissi helps us realize we are not by ourselves. God is directing us, battling for us, and here right now. "If God be for us, who can be against us?" Romans 8:31. Our victory is certain in Him; hence, under His banner, no conflict is too great, or opposition is too strong.

Examining the potent legacy of Jehovah Nissi in our own lives requires us to draw motivation from the prophets who have come before us. Often at tremendous personal sacrifice, their lives were evidence of audacious obedience. Still, they stayed strong as they understood God's banner was over them. Their faithfulness cleared the path for subsequent generations, and we are living due to their obedience. We are to live with that same audacity now. God has promised and declared his name as a banner over us and promised to guard and guide us; we are not battling alone. Our job is to keep in line with His will and know that the seeds we sow now will produce fruit for subsequent generations. As He did with the prophets, God utilizes our lives to create a lasting influence, whether in little acts of faith or significant obedience strides.

This confidence drives us to be audacious in our compliance. Knowing Jehovah Nissi comes before us transforms everything. Whether personal, spiritual, or relational, our conflicts are no longer fought from our strength. We battle beneath the flag of the Almighty, the One who has already guaranteed our triumph. Isaiah 54:17 puts it this way: "No weapon that is formed against thee shall prosper, and every tongue that shall rise against thee in judgment Thou shalt condemn." Therefore, our inheritance under Jehovah Nissi is this. It's more than just a sign of God's presence; it's a guarantee that we have already been granted the victory whatsoever that comes our way and a lasting legacy of victory and triumph in Christ.

Whether it was Isaiah, Ezekiel, or Jeremiah, every prophet of God flew the banner of Jehovah Nissi like lighthouses of faith, discipline, and bravery. They were forth-telling the heart of God, bringing people back to Him and reminding them that under His flag, they had nothing to fear; they were not only prophesying the future. Each of us is meant to carry this banner in our own lives. This is a living truth, not only a historical idea for us now. Be encouraged to be vessels through which God's splendor is shown to the world and to enter that same prophetic tradition. Let us not forget that this banner is for us, not only for the prophets of old, as we continue to explore the relevance of Jehovah Nissi.

As a carrier of God's banner, you are invited to boldly announce His truth from within a prophetic legacy spanning time and geography. When your life aligns with His will, you become evidence of His grace and power. Though you can encounter resistance, like the prophets, you can be resolute, knowing that we are more than conquerors beneath the banner of Jehovah Nissi. "Nay, in all these things, we are more than conquerors through him that loved us" (Romans 8:37).

Our calling is obvious; our victory is safe as the Lord our Banner guides us, securely guards us, and guarantees that His desire for us will be carried out. Like the prophets of old, let us stay true to the call God has set upon our lives. May we walk and work knowing that under the banner of Jehovah Nissi, we are part of something everlasting, something far more than ourselves. Knowing that our lives, like those of the prophets, have the power to change the world in which we live permanently, it is only in God's banner that we can live this boldly.

CHAPTER THREE

THE BANNER OVER
OUR LIVES

When we examine the lives of people who carried Jehovah Nissi's banner, few are as significant as Mary, the mother of Jesus. Mary's life is an excellent monument to what it means to live under God's divine banner— a life defined by favor, obedience, and relentless faith. Her path is a beautiful example of what results when we submit to God's will and let His favor direct and guard us.

One cannot underestimate Mary's importance in God's redemptive scheme. God's mercy chose her to carry out the assignment of bearing the Savior of the world, therefore changing the path of human history. But this work called for great trust, bravery, and a heart given to God's plan. A virgin was to be with a child by the Holy Ghost, and the word of the Lord came to Mary; if she hadn't believed and said, "Be it so unto me," then perhaps another virgin would have been favored. But she aligned herself and submitted her life to that sent word.

Mary's story tells us that God prepares us when He calls us, and His banner of safety follows us at every turn of the road. Though she was the only virgin selected by God for this enormous work, Mary was not the only virgin in Israel. This begs an exciting issue for thought. Mary: Why? She distinguished herself from the other young women of her day by something. Her virginity, which was essential to fulfill the prophecy, is only one aspect; her heart condition and close relationship with God also play a part. Mary was ready for the scope of her calling.

"Hail Mary, Thou art highly favored; the Lord is with thee; blessed art Thou among women." Luke 1:28 notes the greeting the angel Gabriel extends to Mary. This salutation emphasizes Mary's favor from God, although this favor was not bestowed by happenstance. It was a mirror of Mary's openness to welcome God's divine design for her life. God sensed her heart, loyalty, and desire to say "yes" even in doubt. Mary responded to the angel's message quite remarkably. She modestly states in Luke 1:38, "Behold the handmaid of the Lord; be it unto me according to thy word." This reply is what exposed her wholehearted compliance with God's will. It's a profound expression of trust in God's plan, not only an embrace of her calling.

Mary must have recognized that following God's will would present difficulties, but she would be shielded and guided under Jehovah Nissi's banner. Her story reminds us that navigating under God's banner does not mean we will not encounter challenges. Instead, it implies that His favor will envelop us and His presence will precede us in whatever circumstance. Mary's character is much shown by her readiness to accept her responsibility and calling despite personal difficulties and social consequences.

In her society, unmarried pregnancy might have resulted in public humiliation, rejection, and even death. Mary, however, refused to let her dread of what others might say stop her from doing what God had called. Her bravery in such overwhelming circumstances perfectly illustrates what it means to believe in God's will. Knowing that God is with us, battling for us, and covering us with His favor when we walk under Jehovah Nissi's banner should comfort and strengthen you so that we, too, may face the challenges ahead with bravery.

Perhaps Mary's capacity to accept and serve God's will was much enhanced by her familiarity with the scriptures or being a prophet follower. One will more readily believe that she was a vessel (unto honor) selected for her spiritual readiness as much as for her purity. In many respects, Mary was a walking Bible. Often referred to as the Magnificent, her song of gratitude in Luke 1:46–55 contains Old Testament biblical references. This exposes a heart aligned with God's will even before the angel showed her, one entrenched in the Word of God.

Given her spiritual profundity, Mary was the perfect vehicle for the Word, Jesus, to enter the flesh. This emphasizes a crucial reality shared by all of us: God sees not just our external credentials. He studies our hearts, faith, and readiness to live according to His Word. Mary was the ideal candidate to be the Savior's mother because she closely followed God's will. She was not qualified for such a great calling by her position, riches, or earthly success. She distinguished herself with her close relationship with God and thorough awareness of His Word. God is not seeking perfection when He calls us to walk under His banner. He is searching for hearts prepared to say, "Let it be unto me according to Your Word," those turned to Him.

Mary's story reminds us that, even in incomplete knowledge, walking under the banner of Jehovah Nissi means trusting God's plan. It entails faith that His favor will suffice to get us through the difficulties and demands of obeying His will. Like Mary, we can walk confidently, knowing that God has already gone before us, even though we may not know all the specifics of the road forward. We can say, "The Lord is my light and my salvation; whom shall I fear?" Just as the psalmist asks? We can declare, of whom shall I be terrified? The Lord is the strength of my life.

Sometimes, God urges you to enter something that feels beyond your reach. The enormity of what God asks of you could make you feel unworthy, unprepared, or overburdened. In those times, let Mary's story remind you that God's banner is above you, and His favor will direct and guard you in whatever circumstance. Let your heart become conduits for His glory to be shown in the world when you align with His will. Knowing that you are more than conquerors under Jehovah Nissi's banner, therefore, like Mary, you can enter your life's calling bravely.

Our Role In God's Plan

We are called to live under the banner of Jehovah Nissi, just as Mary was named. Like Mary, our ability to fulfill our particular part in God's great plan will rely on our alignment with his will. Living under God's banner is about letting go of our will and orienting ourselves to fit His use. It is about availability and eagerness more than perfection. God searches for willing vessels, those who can honestly say, "I am the Lord's servant; be it unto me according to thy word," not necessarily for perfect vessels (Luke 1:38). Such a statement's simplicity and power show how trust and preparation define alignment with God's will rather than having all the answers.

Also, our relationship with God mainly determines our position in His plan. We connect more precisely with His heart the more we sink ourselves into His Word and presence. Like Mary, we must be spiritually ready and attentive when God calls. God's banner above us is a banner of favor and purpose as much as a protection from peril. Living under this divine protection helps us to be able to complete the tasks God has assigned us. Mary's story reminds us that God's banner is a proactive proclamation of His purpose rather than only a passive kind of protection and also shows us our part in it.

Like Mary, the road of faith is one of unknowns, hardships, and hazards. But during these times, we have to remember that God's banner marks triumph. Jehovah Nissi is the God who has already emerged victorious, not only the one who battles for us. Like Mary's, our job is to stay in line with His will and rely on His plan even if the way looks unknown.

Moreover, knowing that God's plan and time are always perfect and His ways are more significant than ours helps us to find serenity. Living under His banner means that, since He has already conquered, we are not just fighters but also winners. As we negotiate life's difficulties, we must realize that our part in God's design is far from passive. Like Mary, who is actively engaged in God's redemptive scheme, so must we. We must be ready and eager to answer God's call with obedience and confidence. We cannot afford to be passive or bystanders. This calls for a constant dependence on God's direction and a strong will toward spiritual development.

We understand that her spiritual preparedness, understanding of scripture, and following influenced God's selection of Mary. Similarly, we must develop our spiritual strength since the more we climb on our path of faith, the more we depend on God's banner for defense. The enemy will surely try to impede our advancement, but under Jehovah Nissi, we are convinced that "no weapon formed against thee shall prosper" (Isaiah 54:17).

It is also our role to understand that coming under the flag of Jehovah Nissi also means realizing that our life is a part of something much more than we could know. Mary's obedience transformed her personal life and the whole direction of human history. Similarly, our compliance with God could affect life and mold destinies in ways we would never appreciate entirely. When we follow God's will, our deeds help His more excellent intentions on earth pass. Though we might not always see the whole picture, our compliance can set off waves of change affecting many lives, much as Mary's "yes" resulted in the birth of the Savior.

Mary's readiness to carry the weight of her calling despite uncertainty and hazards reveals that alignment with God's intention has long-lasting effects. Though under Jehovah Nissi's banner, we can be sure that our efforts support a far-reaching plan beyond our lifetime, even though we may not always witness the direct result of our compliance. Mary's life reminds us that following God's will always result in purpose; when that purpose aligns with God's will, there is transformation, not only in our own lives but in the lives of people around us.

Under the banner of Jehovah Nissi, our role is a call to walk in faith, believe in God's favor, and line up with His divine intent. Like Mary, we are expected to be vessels of His glory, ready to enter whatever position He has assigned us. Though we never know the result, we can relax because Jehovah Nissi has already guaranteed our success. As we follow His banner, let us remember that our obedience can mold destinies and transform lives, much as Mary's faithfulness revealed the Savior of the world.

Trusting In God's Timing

Trusting in God's timing is among the most challenging things about living under His banner. The life of Mary is the ideal example of this. Now, we know that the angel's message to Mary was a promise involving waiting, perseverance, and patience rather than a one-time occurrence that immediately altered her life. She was told she would birth the Savior, but the road she traveled was anything but simple. Mary had to go through the physical trip to Bethlehem, social censure, and even the everyday challenges of pregnancy. Though it was hardly the ideal scenario, birthing in a modest stable was all in the perfect timing for God.

Every turn Mary took on her path tested her faith, and every test showed her steadfast faith in God's will. Many of us would have questioned and murmured why the God who created heaven and earth would let us give birth in a manger. And often, in our lives, we experience comparable seasons of waiting. However, the things God promises us, whether through scripture, prayer, or prophetic utterances, do not always appear immediately. This waiting time is preparation time rather than an absence of activity. We, too, have to get ready during our seasons of waiting, much as Mary did emotionally and spiritually for the great responsibility of raising Jesus. Believing in God's timing calls us to be obedient even if the result is not yet apparent.

Under the banner of Jehovah Nissi, His protection covers us, yet we are also urged to believe that His promises will be kept in His perfect timing. Romans 8:28 informs us of this: "And we know that all things work together for good to them that love God, to them who are the called according to his purpose." Though it seems like a test of endurance, waiting is a spiritual development and alignment phase. God helps us develop our character, strengthen our faith, and prepare for His promised fulfillment throughout these times. Mary's story teaches us that waiting is crucial in following God's will; it is not a sign of weakness. Her struggles, like riding on a donkey when heavily pregnant, unsure about where she would deliver, were all part of a greater narrative. And, like in Mary's situation, our waiting times and hardships fit a larger story.

God sees the complete picture, and His timing is always perfect, even if, from the start, we cannot see the finish. Living under the flag of Jehovah Nissi is ultimately about more than just getting God's protection; it's about bringing our lives into line with His will and depending on His timetable. In the waiting, we are being polished and ready for more significant events. Mary fulfilled her part in God's plan and left a legacy for the next generations through her faith, obedience, and thorough knowledge of God's Word. Her readiness to follow God's will and trust His timing finally produced the Savior, a turning point in history.

When we consider Mary's example, let's be motivated to live under the banner of Jehovah Nissi, therefore embracing God's will for our lives with faith and compliance. This banner signifies that we are part of a greater good that could call for waiting, tenacity, and even pain, not only protection. But, just as Mary trusted God on her path, so too may we believe He will carry His promises to pass in our lives. Knowing that He already guarantees our triumph and that everything works together for our good, let us rely on His timing. And let us remember that, like Mary, our life fits into a far grander plan.

The waiting period is not wasted time as we negotiate our paths of faith. It's time for you to get to work while you wait. Mary waited and mastered trust in God's timing; similarly, we are being molded and ready for the fulfillment of God's promises in our lives. We are called to be obedient, believe in God's will, and remember that Jehovah Nissi's banner is before us, guiding and defending us. God is arranging events in this divine timing, guiding our future, and completing His will in ways beyond human understanding. Believing in Jehovah Nissi means believing His timing is always flawless, His plan is always more significant, and His promises never fail.

CHAPTER FOUR

VICTORY AMID TRIALS

Among the most gripping stories in the Bible, Esther's story eloquently illustrates the authority and protection of God's banner over His people. From being an orphan to rising to being a queen, Esther's story illustrates how God works behind the scenes to match His people with His divine will. Born in exile, distant from any prospect of fame or majesty, her background was modest, her future unknown, but none of these elements stopped God from manifesting the glory of being beneath His banner at the ideal moment.

The apparent lesson Esther's path reminds us is that if we stay in line with God's will, He can raise us to areas of power from anywhere we begin. This is the core of Jehovah Nissi, the Lord, our Banner, working behind the scenes to coordinate events we might not completely understand, which are vital to His divine design. Esther's change from obscurity to monarchy resulted from God's sovereign hand guiding her into a sphere of authority; it was not a coincidence. God had set her out for a very particular reason, even if, at first, she might not have realized the whole weight of her position. Her ascent to popularity was driven by personal comfort or benefit and the defense of her people.

Esther's story is a potent illustration of how Jehovah Nissi strives to place us where we belong, even when the journey seems unknown or the obstacles seem insurmountable. Her cousin Mordecai says the remarkable lines, "And who knoweth whether thou art come to the kingdom for such a time as this?" in Esther 4:14. This question speaks to us since it reminds us that we, too, are frequently set in our path for purposes much beyond our awareness. Though under God's banner, Esther found both safety and purpose, her ascent was beset with difficulties.

Esther might have initially decided to retreat from fear. Approaching the king uninvited might have cost her life, and she carried the weight of her people's existence. Still, Esther decided to believe the God who had crowned her queen despite her fear. Apart from providing protection, the Jehovah Nissi banner helps us to act when the stakes are significant against us and even when they seemingly appear to be in our favor, but God knows best. Esther's choice to venture with faith in the face of risk captures the bravery resulting from knowing God is with us.

With God as your banner, no matter how complex the tasks He has assigned you are, He prepares you to play the roles He has called you to. Esther's story reveals a vital truth: under God's banner, no enemy is too intense, no task too severe, and no circumstance too bleak. Esther could have easily remained silent, hiding under significant risk in protecting her royal post. She knew, though, that her position as queen was divinely arranged for the release of her people, not only for her advantage. Her conduct sprang from this knowledge. Esther's narrative reminds us that God's banner is a call to rise boldly and serve the reason for which we have been positioned, not merely a sign of security.

Under God's banner, we are ready to overcome, even though, like Esther, we are frequently in situations that call for faith, action, and courage. Esther's story is beautiful in its relentless faith in God's timing and intent. She trusted the One who had placed her there, even if she might not have realized precisely how her activities would result in success. She discovered the will to intervene for her people under the banner of Jehovah Nissi, risking all to carry out the destiny God had assigned her. Those under God's banner differ from others in this degree of confidence and obedience. We are invited to get His protection and live in His purpose with trust, knowing that every action contributes to a more excellent, divine design.

This is an excellent monument to how God acts in our lives, orienting us in places of influence and significance even in the least expected direction. Her life shows that God's banner is a divine covering that helps us to rise to the occasion, no matter how overwhelming the circumstances may seem, and is not only a protection from harm. Esther was called to save her people; we, too, are called to occupy the roles God has set for us, confident that we are qualified to serve our divine purpose under His banner. As stated in Isaiah 54:17, "No weapon that is formed against thee shall prosper." Knowing that His safety, purpose, and victory are guaranteed, this promise is the banner we fly as we enter the unique positions God puts us in.

Jehovah Nissi In Our Trials

Like Esther, we are summoned to stand beneath God's banner throughout her ordeal. Life presents various difficulties, including illness, financial hardships, relationship problems, and spiritual strife. Under these circumstances, Jehovah Nissi, the Lord our Banner, battles for us, stands before us and guarantees our triumph. His banner reminds us constantly that we are not alone. It names His heavenly protection, love, and authority over our lives.

This comfort should remind you that God is constantly battling on your behalf and should fortify you when you feel weak. When tests and trials arise, one naturally feels overwhelmed or even discouraged. Esther's narrative reminds us that our challenges are meant to expose God's might and faithfulness rather than to break us. Though Esther had great difficulties, God's glory was shown through tribulations.

Our challenges sometimes serve as the furnace where our faith is polished, and we grow to have more thorough trust in Jehovah Nissi. The challenges we face highlight God's promise to work all things for our good, like stepping stones toward success. "And we know that all things work together for good to them that love God, to them who are called according to his purpose," Romans 8:28.

The Book of Esther is unique since it never specifically names God by name, yet His presence is sensed in every moment. This is a sobering lesson for us: sometimes, God's work in our lives is not immediately apparent. Though we could pass seasons when we feel His presence absent, this does not mean He is not present. He silently and powerfully guides us under His banner every step of the way, much as He coordinates events behind Esther's life.

Trusting In God's Sovereignty

Esther's narrative teaches us, among other essential things, the need to trust in God's sovereignty, even in cases of incomplete understanding of His plan. Given that the penalty for approaching the king without a summons could have been death, Esther's first hesitation was reasonable and understandable. Still, she believed her life belonged to the God who had brought her to that pivotal point. Her proclamation, "If I perish, I perish" (Esther 4:16), shows her preparedness to follow regardless of the result and powerfully expresses faith and resignation to God's purpose.

In our struggles, we are also called to believe in God's sovereignty, and many times, we need to verbalize our resolve and commitment to push through. There will be times when the road ahead looks uncertain, the hazards seem too intense, and the stakes seem extreme. But these very times, we must ground our faith in Jehovah Nissi, the God who sees the end from the beginning and owns every element of our life.

Though we cannot see it, he is actively trying to guarantee our success; he is not remote. Trusting in God's sovereignty is about acting actively rather than being passive. It entails believing that God's plans for us are good and progressing in compliance, even if the result is unknown. Knowing that God's banner above us is one of love, protection, and triumph, we are invited to face our trials with trust, taking lessons from Esther, who responded with bravery.

Victory Through Obedience

Esther's victory came from her response to God's summons at the right moment, not her title as queen. She chose to play the part God had meant for her rather than staying mute and hiding herself behind her regal title. This act of faith and obedience saved her people and guaranteed she would be seen as a brave and devout woman. Her story shows that even if it is challenging, the only path to reach true success is to be ready to move outside our comfort zones and follow the direction of God.

Usually, the areas of our lives where we struggle most to follow God are the ones in which we find the most success when we obey Him. One is shown God's protection and favor when confronted with risk and uncertainty. When we decide to follow, we enable His power to run through us and bring ourselves into line with the divine purpose God wants for us.

As Esther's obedience led to the freedom of the Jews, so too can our obedience produce discoveries that help and affect those around us. Jehovah Nissi has made us more than conquerors, even if the obstacles we face occasionally seem beyond us. The success of our lives depends on our preparedness to believe in and follow God, not on our powers. Like Esther, we could find ourselves in circumstances when the chances are stacked against us; yet, when we fly under the banner of God, we can have peace of mind knowing that He has already guaranteed our success. Our strength is not what guarantees success; instead, His strength does.

The Power Of Intercession

Esther's story emphasizes the great authority intercession can create. Esther did not act quickly; instead, she asked for a period of fasting and prayer before approaching the king to ask for her people (Esther 4:16). She knew she had a significant influence on the result. Still, she also knew God would finally decide the outcome. Through group prayer and heavenly intervention, Esther brought her people and herself into line with God's intention. This mediation was about urging God to work through the unity of His people so that His hand might control the events that were to follow, not only about her bravery.

For us these days, intercession is still a potent weapon. Though, just like Esther, we are urged to gather in prayer and present our troubles to Jehovah Nissi, it is easy to experience emotions of loneliness or being overwhelmed by the challenges we face and protesting ourselves before God in the name of intercessmediation to realize that the challenge is not only for us. We enter the more prominent spiritual family, where our voices join to pray for the expression of God's power in our life here on Earth.

Intercession is about orienting ourselves with God's will and asking His divine protection and intervention in our circumstances, not only about a call for help. As we go through the obstacles life confronts us with, Esther, a woman who decided to stand firm beneath the flag of God while overcome with dread and uncertainty, might be our model. Esther experienced the remarkable deliverance that God had given by walking in obedience, seeking His face through prayer, and believing in His timing. As Esther did, knowing that Jehovah Nissi is standing before us guarantees success on our behalf and gives us the bravery and strength required.

Indeed, when living beneath His banner, we are more than conquerors. Esther's narrative is not simply a collection of historical events but also a convincing illustration of the power God has to operate through those who believe in Him. Her story reminds us that we may bring God's victory into our lives by aligning ourselves with God's goal for us, remaining obedient, and participating in mediation, transcending our obstacles. Like Esther, I pray we might stick to Jehovah Nissi's and believe in His developed strategy. God is guiding and safeguarding us; thus, we can have hope that even the most demanding challenges will lead to fantastic rescue and the realization of His will for our generation.

CHAPTER FIVE

LIVING UNDER THE BANNER OF JEHOVAH NISSI

Walking the road needed to live under the banner of Jehovah Nissi requires a faith more than surface-level faith; it requires a tremendous and lasting maturity in the things that God has and spiritual realities. This ought to be a wake-up call. In his letter to the Corinthians in 1 Corinthians 6:19–20, the apostle Paul charges us to recognize the cost paid for our atonement. He says you are not your own; you were bought at a price. Honor God with your bodies, then. This proclamation reminds us profoundly that God is the owner of our whole being, including our spirit, soul, and body, and so this is not only to inspire us to be holy in the physical sense.

Living under His banner is an all-encompassing commitment that calls for us to grow above our present level in discernment and keep alert in our spiritual lives. Though faced with the most challenging conditions, Paul's life offers the best picture of what it means to live under the banner of Jehovah Nissi. He suffered great persecution, several incarcerations, and numerous physical illnesses throughout his journey.

Paul's dedication to his cause never wavered during all these years.

He saw that his life had been utterly submitted to God's will rather than his own. It presented a chance for him to show Jehovah Nissi's strength, grace, and faithfulness in every challenge he encountered. Paul's life illustrates how our response to difficulty, which shields us under God's protection and direction, defines our spiritual development rather than the absence of difficulty.

The call to maturity is more crucial than ever in this day and age when there are many distractions, and the stresses of life can often cause us to stray from our path. It is not enough to only be familiar with the Bible; instead, we must also apply the lessons of God's Word to every aspect of our lives to acquire a degree of spiritual maturity. It suggests having the capacity to have confidence in Jehovah Nissi even if our environment seems to contradict those promises, to keep one's faith even when others stumble, and to identify the voice of God even in the middle of turbulence.

Should we live beneath this holy banner, we must also be alert. 1 Peter 5:8 states that the enemy is always searching for innocent people to devour. He is aware that young believers or people, in terms of their spiritual growth, are more prone to be victims of his fraud. This means that, as Christ's disciples, we have to equip ourselves with the whole armor of God (Ephesians 6:11–18), which comprises constantly refreshing our minds with the truth revealed in the Word of God and vigilance and praying. Being mature in Christ helps us to see the tactics used by the enemy and to keep our hearts and minds safe in awareness that the banner of Jehovah Nissi shields us.

Our Response To God's Banner

Underneath the Jehovah Nissi banner, we must actively and deliberately respond; it is not a passive experience. This holy banner requires our surrender to His will, even as it marks God's love, protection, and victory. Though the road ahead looks challenging or unknown, this surrender is a daily commitment to trust God's leadership rather than a one-time choice. It's about aligning our will with His moment by moment, decision by decision, choice after choice.

Think of the life of the apostle Paul as a model for this kind of whole submission. Paul's answer was always unflinching confidence and trust in God despite many challenges, including imprisonments, beatings, shipwrecks, and continuous resistance. He welcomed these challenges as chances to show the force of God operating in him, not only enduring them. Paul's fantastic proclamation, "I have learned to be content whatever the circumstances" (Philippians 4:11), sprang from a profound, abiding faith in Jehovah Nissi rather than easy living. Paul's contentment was derived from his relationship with Jehovah Nissi, who had found him, equipped him, and pledged to be with him through every difficulty; it had nothing to do with his often terrible circumstances. So, Paul's life reminds us that while living under God's banner guarantees a purposeful life full of chances to show God's power and grace, it does not guarantee an easy one.

A solid dedication to prayer must also mark our response to life under God's banner. Prayer is not only a religious obligation; it's our connection to the Father, the way we match ourselves with His will and get the strength we need to meet the demands of daily life. Praying helps us find serenity amid turbulence and apparent uncertainty and gain power in weakness. Often withdrawing to converse with the Father, Jesus Himself lived a life of perpetual prayer, frequently alone (Luke 5:16). If the Son of God, who is flawless and sinless, had to give prayer a top priority, how much more do we, in our limited knowledge and frailty, need to make prayer a pillar of our life?

Prayer is beyond the least we can do; it's the most effective action. Apart from prayer, our reaction to Jehovah Nissi's banner must be a dedication to learning and meditation on God's Word. The Bible is God's living, active Word, full of promises and directions we need to live our lives under His banner, not only a book of ancient wisdom. "Your word is a lamp for my feet, a light on my path," Psalm 119:105 so brilliantly states. God's Word offers relentless truth and direction in a society full of competing voices and changing ideals.

Immersion in Scripture helps us acquire the wisdom and insight required to make virtuous decisions, avoid temptation, and stay rooted in the truth of who we are in Christ. Our offensive weapon in spiritual battle is the Word of God, the sword of the Spirit, which cuts through lies and bolsters our faith. For people under God's banner, regular, profound interaction with Scripture is not optional but essential.

Another essential component of living under God's banner is walking in compliance. Obedience is the evidence of our love for God and our faith in His sovereignty, not about minding a set of laws. When the road is clear, and the cost is modest, it's straightforward to follow, yet absolute obedience is tested in the furnace of challenge. Our faith is shown real in those times of decision when faithfulness costs us something. Our ultimate model, Jesus, showed complete obedience even to death on the cross (Philippians 2:8). His obedience came from His love for the Father and us; it was not grudgingly or unwillingly.

With this obedience, sin and death were defeated, bringing about the biggest triumph the planet has ever known. Likewise, our compliance with God's will sets us to see His triumph in our lives. Under Jehovah Nissi, life is about advancement rather than perfection. It's about developing our confidence, deepening our prayer practice, learning God's Word, and improving our obedience. We will discover as we do this that we are standing solid, walking with more assurance, and noticing more of God's power in our lives. Under His banner, we are more than conquerors; we are overcomers, thanks to Him who loved us.

The Assurance Of Victory

The banner of Jehovah Nissi over us serves as a solid and continual reminder that our problems are never isolated. The wars we fight are not waged in our strength; instead, they are fought with the Lord Himself before us, guaranteeing triumph on our behalf. Exodus 17 illustrates this truth amid the struggle between the Israelites and the Amalekites. Moses stood atop the hill, clutching the staff of God. The Israelites won as long as his hands were lifted. But the Amalekites started to take the stage when he felt tired and dropped them. Understanding the need for Moses's hands to be raised, Aaron and Hur accompanied him to encourage him so he might keep intervening and bring Israel's victory (Exodus 17:11–13). Following this miraculous triumph, Moses erected an altar named Jehovah Nissi, meaning "The Lord is my Banner" (Exodus 17:15).

This moment sums up the Israelites' experience: their triumph resulted from God's divine intervention rather than their military might. Moses relied on God's power, which he represented by raising his hands, therefore winning the battle. This event strongly reminds us that God is our banner, behind which we can discover strength, defense, and success. The narrative of Moses raising his hands imparts a vital lesson: our victory depends on our reliance on God, not on our capacity or efforts alone. We must ultimately rely on Jehovah Nissi during our battles, just as Moses relied on God to guarantee the triumph for Israel.

Under God's banner, we are sheltered by His might, whether our obstacles are spiritual warfare, emotional struggles, or personal. His banner signifies victory as much as love and protection. Sometimes in life, the fight seems too fierce, and its weight becomes intolerable. These are the times when, like Moses, we could feel tired. But God places people in our lives to uplift us, pray for us, and remind us that we do not have to fight alone. Just as Aaron and Hur supported Moses, he sent us men as divine helpers.

Under Jehovah Nissi, we are members of a greater community of believers who support and pray with us. We can confront any struggle with confidence when we live in obedience, trust God's sovereignty, and align ourselves with His purposes. Victory comes from God's promise to fight for us while we hold our peace, not from our will or knowledge. Jehovah Nissi's banner is a powerful conviction that guarantees the Lord has already secured the outcome regardless of how fierce the fight is.

The Role Of Community

Living under Jehovah's Nissi banner also helps one realize the great value of community. In Moses's story, the triumph over the Amalekites was secured not just by his faith or will but also by something else: Aaron and Hur's encouragement, which kept his hands lifted as he grew tired. They were by his side. This picture reminds me strongly of how God intended us to live, not in solitude but in fellowship with others.

Our spiritual community provides the strength and encouragement we need, much as Moses needed the help of all around him. Not only is it a choice, but our spiritual well-being depends on being a part of a community of believers. Galatians 6:2 encourages us to "bear ye one another's burdens, and so fulfill the law of Christ." This is a call to support one another during the trials and conflicts of life. Whether by prayer, words of support, or doable deeds of kindness, we owe it to one another to uplift.

The banner of Jehovah Nissi above us represents His protection and gift of a spiritual family to walk with us across every difficulty. The New Testament stresses this point of view constantly. In Hebrews 10:24–25, we are urged to "consider one another to provoke unto love and to good works" and "not forsake the assembling of ourselves together." These songs stress the power derived from oneness. Under God's banner, we are part of a more significant body, the church, who are called to stand together, encourage one another, and be a lighthouse in one another's life—not just people fighting our battles in isolation.

Living under Jehovah Nissi means realizing the great weapons we possess in love, unity, and friendship. The enemy could try to separate us, but when we stand together, his plans are undermined. Reflecting the heart of Jehovah Nissi, our protection is in our oneness and love for one another. We know our successes come from standing together under God's great banner rather than fighting alone.

Walking In Victory

Walking in victory every day we live is to embrace the banner of Jehovah Nissi and dwell beneath it. Conversely, the expression of this triumph does not always follow outward or apparent lines. Instead, it is a great inner confidence, a firm conviction that, whatever the challenges we are faced with, we are "more than conquerors through Him that loved us" (Romans 8:37). When we talk about faith, we mean the calm conviction that God's purposes for our life will always prevail, independent of how overwhelming the situation may seem to be. The banner He has flown over us represents the reality that His protection covers all around us, His love shields us, and His power keeps us going through any stage of life.

We know better what it means to live under Christ's banner as our faith develops and our relationship with God deepens. We arrive at this knowledge using a life of prayer, immersion in His Word, and obedience, walking in line with His direction. We are living a thriving life, not only existing, which we are constantly overcoming. Under Jehovah Nissi, Christ has given us authority and strength to help us advance the Kingdom of God. This life is meant for us to embrace our divine calling and enter the fullness of God's promises, knowing that we are correctly ready to win.

Moreover, living under the banner of Jehovah Nissi is about

honoring God with our victories, not only about reaching personal excellence. When we follow His will and live in line with it, we show His majesty to the world around us and offer ourselves prosperity. Using this victorious life, we might reflect on His glory and expose the transforming force of His love and grace to others. Given this, let us promise to live under the banner of Jehovah Nissi totally and completely.

This complete faith allows us to be convinced the Lord is with us, that He is for us, and that He has already guaranteed our victory. Giving in to this reality helps us live our lives with bravery and confidence, therefore completing the heavenly goals we have been assigned. With every step we take, we will honor God; His banner will always remind us that we are never apart from one another and that success is always assured. May we be found faithful under the banner of the Lord our God, now and always. Amen.

CHAPTER SIX

THE TRIUMPH IS OURS

We become unstoppable when we reach this great truth —the triumph is ours. Jehovah Nissi assures us that we are never alone in every fight, difficulty, or moment of doubt. Rising high above our lives, his banner declares divine triumph, divine victory already assured for us. Our strength or knowledge does not define this victory; it is anchored in God's unquestionable love and power.

Jehovah Nissi's banner signifies God's constant support and direction in our lives, much as a banner in war denotes the presence and protection of the leader. God has shown Himself faithful right from the start. Moses's hands raised as he stood on the hill marked a physical gesture and a spiritual proclamation that the Lord owned the fight. Jehovah Nissi fought on behalf of the Israelites; hence, their victory over the Amalekites resulted from their backing rather than their strength or strategic endeavors.

This reminds us that in our own lives, our human efforts alone cannot define success. God enters our situations, and His intervention results in the victory we yearn for. Like Moses, we are invited to raise our hands in surrender and realize the Lord is the source of our power. And so it is right now. The same God who gave Moses conquest also keeps giving His people triumph. Whether spiritual, emotional, or bodily, we can be sure that Jehovah Nissi works for us in our challenges. His banner of love and protection reminds us that we are not battling alone.

Though the demands of life might easily overwhelm us, the truth is that God is always present, working behind the scenes to guarantee our success. Our part is to keep raising our hands in confidence as Moses did and to trust in His faithfulness. The banner of Jehovah Nissi announces that we are under divine protection rather than only denoting success. God is thus in charge, regardless of how intense the fight seems. Seeing the finish from the beginning, he knows how to guide us to success. Our job is to walk in trust and obedience under His banner.

Knowing God is our banner will help us boldly and confidently negotiate life's challenges. Though we never know exactly how success will arrive, we can certainly be sure it is already guaranteed as a Jehovah Nissi victory for us. Thus, consider Jehovah Nissi's importance in our lives and take courage. Our fights now are only opportunities for God to prove Himself strong on our side; they are not meant to defeat us. Trusting the Lord our Banner to be before us, let us raise our hands in surrender and faith, as Moses did. Victory is inevitable because of who God is. He is faithful, mighty, and always present. It is not because of what we have done. Jehovah Nissi is with us; constantly, we will overcome through Him.

Living In The Reality Of Divine Triumph

The lives of biblical leaders, including Moses, Esther, Mary, and Paul, are not only historical narratives; they are illustrations of what happens when we come together under the banner of Jehovah Nissi. These people knew their hardships were not only their own; hence, they could triumph even if they faced significant challenges. These incidents belonged to a divine narrative in which God Himself was the author and the one finishing the story, too.

This same reality connects to us now. When faced with

challenges, it is crucial to remember that we are not fighting alone; instead, we are a part of a more remarkable story God is guiding to glorify Himself. Moses, for example, was able to release a country from slavery, but he accomplished this using God's might rather than his own. His confidence in God's direction derived from his ability to effectively negotiate his path from a shy leader to the one separating the Red Sea. In the same vein, Esther accepted the call of God even though she was endangering her own life, saving her people from extinction rather than because of her royal status. Her bravery came from knowing God had placed her in a position to save her people. These stories show that our flaws don't get in the way of God's plan when we accept it.

God chose and preferred Mary, Jesus' mother, so that she could have the Savior of the world. It wasn't because she was competent in and of herself. Her story tells us that when God's favor is on us, there may be problems. But because we are under His banner, those problems make it possible for His promises to come true; they become stepping stones instead of stumbling blocks.

Despite persecution and suffering, Paul brought the gospel to every corner of the world since he lived under Christ's victory. The fact that he never wavered in his faith, even in the face of significant obstacles, showcases how the banner of God gives us the means to keep moving and overcome. These events have been put in our lives to tell us we are part of this incredible story. We are not just watching God's success happen; we are actively involved in it. Our lives are intricately connected to His grand plan, and the banner He unequivocally raises over us proclaims love, safety, and victory! In times of trouble, may you find comfort in knowing that Jehovah Nissi, the Lord your Banner, is with you, fighting for you and leading you to victory.

The Assurance Of Triumph In Christ

Jesus Christ is the best way Jehovah Nissi expresses itself. Christ carried the entire weight of sin, death, and the powers of darkness on the cross. Jesus hanging on the cross, forsaken and hated—what seemed to be a moment of defeat—was the most significant victory in history. In His dying words, "It is finished," Christ was not merely declaring His life to be ending. He was saying that the task of securing our future triumph was finished. For everyone who would ever call upon His name, this victory was not only for that instant but all eternity. It was a triumph over sin, death, and the adversary's will.

To appreciate the intensity of this victory, picture a courtroom scene. Before God, humanity stands guilty with an overwhelming list of offenses against us. Death is the penalty for our sin; yet, just as the sentence is about to be administered, Jesus steps forward and says, "I've paid it all." Christ's sacrifice cleans our debt in that moment, not because of anything we have done but because of him. Jehovah Nissi has a power like this. Now, we walk in Christ's victory on the cross; the fight was fought and won on our behalf. Christ helps us to be more than conquerors—Romans 8:37.

Our triumph is not based on our circumstances, power, or intelligence; it is anchored in the accomplished work of Christ. Paul could, therefore, boldly exclaim, "Thanks be to God, who always leads us in triumphal procession in Christ," despite persecution, shipwrecks, and imprisonment (2 Corinthians 2:14). Though Paul's life presented obstacles that might have easily destroyed him, his knowledge of Christ's victory helped him to transcend every difficulty. Christ had already won the ultimate fight, he realized, regardless of what he confronted.

A typical illustrative example of this can be found in the life of a marathon runner. Imagine a runner in the front of a race. They know they have already won before the gun ever fires. What then? Because someone ran the race for them, surmounted every challenge, and crossed the finish line under their name. All the runner has to do is finish the course, knowing that success is already theirs. Under the banner of Jehovah Nissi, we spend our lives this way. Christ achieved our triumph, overcame the opponent, and already completed the race. We are just living out that triumph; the result is already determined to our advantage.

Living beneath the banner of Christ's triumph has beauty. He has already emerged victorious; we are invited to celebrate His triumph. We are witnesses to God's might at work in our lives, much as the Israelites marveled as the Red Sea opened out before them. We fight from a point of success; we do not have to battle for success. No matter the battles we face, whether financial struggles, health crises, or personal challenges, our triumph is assured because it is Christ's triumph. Knowing that Jehovah Nissi, the Lord our Banner, has already assured us of victory, we walk in His glory when we trust Him.

Embracing Our Role In God's Story

As we walk beneath God's banner, we are thus honoring His love, protection, and might, just as troops march under their flag, symbolizing the authority and defense of their country. Our lives are not arbitrary or insignificant; we are part of a divine purpose. Whether it's an emotional conflict, a spiritual difficulty, or a physical barrier, every fight we go through has greater significance since God guides our lives' events for His will. We must not only be aware of this, but we must embrace it as our role in showcasing God's goodness.

This means we can believe that our life is a part of something far more than we can see, even if the route is challenging. Imagine a wool artwork being created. We all know a jumble of knots, twisted strands, and haphazard designs from the underside. From above, though, the exquisite pattern is evident. Living under Jehovah Nissi's banner is like seeing our life from God's vantage point. God sees the completed design, while we may only see the knots and tangles in the middle of our troubles. He understands how every conflict, every victory, and every moment of difficulty fits the masterwork He is writing for each of us.

Although we might not always follow the road God guides us on, we can be sure His banner over us is love (Song of Solomon 2:4). This is a great truth.

God's banner serves as our shield, much as a shepherd covers his sheep like a little child playing outside in the sweltering heat while their father covers them with an umbrella to provide some relief. Though the youngster might not completely comprehend the need for the umbrella, they naturally believe their father is shielding them. Similarly, although we might not always understand the reason for every trial, we can rely on God to gently cover, guard, and lead us across.

This banner represents realities we may live with daily and is not only a symbol. In a war situation where the general's flag is still clearly visible on the hilltop, it alerts the troops that their leader is still in command. You can only imagine the confidence, authority, and faith instilled in the warriors. Likewise, Jehovah Nissi's banner stays over us as a sign that we are not abandoned in our efforts. Like He did for Moses and the Israelites in their struggles, God fights for us, leads us, and guarantees our triumph.

To enjoy living under this banner, you must believe in God's timing, even if the journey is lengthy and complex. Save yourself the stress of fear, worry, and anxiety. Sometimes, the triumph is not instantaneous; we may feel like Moses in the wilderness, waiting and wondering when the promise will be kept. Living under Jehovah Nissi, however, involves clinging to the hope that God's timing is exactly right. The Israelites beat their enemies in God's time and with His power, not their own. In the same way, your success depends on God's perfect plan, not on your abilities. When you live under Jehovah Nissi's banner, you know you are part of a divine story that ends in victory. Let this give you the courage to live your life.

CONCLUSION

Our Triumph Is Now

L et us proceed with the assurance that triumph is ours, guiding us ahead. Let us walk knowing that Jehovah Nissi, the Lord our Banner, is over us; we can meet life's challenges with conviction and bravery. Though there are many difficulties in life—financial uncertainty, health crises, marital problems—none of them are beyond God's reach. When we stick to our faith, we announce that we believe in a God who has already guaranteed triumph, not only clutching some far-off hope.

Like a soldier in combat who discovers fresh courage and resolve upon witnessing the flag of his country flying high, the banner reminds us that his leader is in charge, that his struggle is not in vain, and that success is within grasp. Likewise, keep your eyes fixed on the Lord's banner to remind you that you are not fighting alone. Jehovah Nissi is in control and is directing you towards success. His presence assures you of something, which gives you the will to keep ahead even if the chances appear stacked against you.

Let us be steadfast in our faith and relentless in our allegiance to God's will. When the road gets difficult or when the triumph appears far off, we may find it easy to lose hope. Everybody has had times when life deviates from expectations. Maybe you are navigating a season of waiting or have prayed for a breakthrough that has not yet materialized. Still, staying steadfast in faith implies trusting God's timing, even if it does not coincide with our own. Consider Abraham, who waited decades for the promise of a son to be realized. Abraham stayed steadfast in his faith despite the long wait since he knew God's promise would come to pass. Ultimately, God honored His word. even amid uncertainty, when we stay dedicated to God's plan and purpose, we place ourselves to experience His promised triumph.

Though you might not see the whole picture right now, like Abraham, your relentless trust will lead to God fulfilling his promises; let your obedience be bold, knowing God's banner over you will never fail. Bold obedience typically entails venturing into the future, risking everything, or following God's direction when it seems illogical by the world's norms. Living under Jehovah Nissi's banner is delightful; nevertheless, as you know, He goes before you, so be unreserved in your allegiance and compliance. His banner promises your security; hence, His love and might shield you even when we enter foreign territories. Imagine Peter, who bravely emerged from the boat and headed for Jesus over the sea. Though brave and horrifying, Peter's obedience was met with supernatural power. He started to sink only as he turned away from Jesus. Similarly, when we keep our attention on God, our bravery in obeying will always be welcomed with His provision and protection.

Sometimes, we lose sight of the whole picture when we are preoccupied with our problems. Living under Jehovah Nissi, however, reminds us that we belong in God's great story. Every moment of success and every difficulty we encounter fits a divine plan in which God's glory serves as the ultimate objective. Our life is not random but carefully spun into His continuous design. The boy Joseph, who went through slavery, jail, and betrayal, could ascend to power in Egypt as a man. Joseph could have asked God why he was suffering at any one moment. Later, Joseph realized God used what his brothers meant for evil (but reasonable) to save many lives. Joseph's life fits a more extensive narrative (that of God), as does our own.

We can relax, aware that God's triumph is the last word, even under trying circumstances. His approach constantly exceeds our current situation. The triumph is a present reality, not only a promise for the future. Right now, among your tribulations, Jehovah Nissi is announcing triumph over your life. Though Christ has already won the war, you might not feel victorious today. Though your present difficulties can become times of heavenly triumph, Christ's death on the cross felt like a defeat, yet it was the most significant victory in history. You are more than just a conqueror under His loving direction (Romans 8:37). Let us thus continue to move forward with this confidence.

Live under the banner of Jehovah Nissi today! Be triumphant in His name, confident in His love, and safe in His protection today! Let this conviction be in you! Though the world may toss its toughest challenges at you, you will be strong knowing that God's banner never fails because those who know their God will be strong and do great exploits! The victory is guaranteed. It is more than a hope. Given who our God is, we already own the triumph. Allow this to be the reality you bring into every situation in your life. And as you live daily, Jehovah Nissi is always your banner; the triumph is yours.

A SPECIAL CALL TO SALVATION & NEW BEGINNINGS FROM APOSTLE DR. DAVID PHILEMON

Dear Beloved,
God loves you deeply and has brought you to this moment for a reason. No matter your past, His love and forgiveness are available to you.

The Bible says in John 3:16, "For God so loved the world that He gave His one and only Son, that whoever believes in Him shall not perish but have eternal life." Jesus Christ came to save you, offering you a new life of purpose and peace.

If you're ready to accept Jesus as your Lord and Savior, pray this simple prayer:

The Salvation Prayer

"Heavenly Father, I come to You in the Name of Jesus. I acknowledge that I am a sinner in need of a Savior. I believe that

Jesus Christ is Your Son, that He died for my sins, and that You raised Him from the dead. I repent of my sins and turn to You with my

Whole heart. Jesus, I ask You to come into my life. Be my Lord and my Savior. I surrender my life to You. Fill me with Your Holy Spirit, guide me on the path of righteousness, and help me to follow Your script for my life. Thank you, Father, for saving me. In the name of Jesus. Amen."

Welcome to the Family of God!

If you have just prayed this prayer, Congratulations! You are now a child of God, and heaven is rejoicing. Your journey has begun, and we're here to support you as you grow in faith and discover God's unique plans for you.

Next Steps:

- Connect with a Bible-believing church.
- Read the Bible Daily: God's Word is your guide.
- Pray Regularly: Prayer is your lifeline to God.
- Share Your Faith: Don't keep the good news to yourself.

ABOUT THE BOOK

This book is about Embracing the name of Jesus of Jehovah Nissi, the Lord our Banner, and having that as a conviction. In it, you will discover how to live brilliantly through every struggle, difficulty, and season of life. This book will enable you to walk courageously in obedience, stand firmly in faith, and experience the surety of God's triumph using inspirational real-life tales, Biblical analogies, and pragmatic insights. If you are ready to enter a life of heavenly success, protection, and purpose, this book is your road map.

www.ingramcontent.com/pod-product-compliance
Lightning Source LLC
Chambersburg PA
CBHW071931020426
42331CB00010B/2814